In loving memory of
the Princess who never became queen
and Rowdy,
who would have been her consort
as well as a budgie named Tiki.

First published by Markosia Enterprises, Ltd, March 2024.
Harry Markos, Director.
www.markosia.com

Illustrations by Nilesh B. Mistry
Book layout by Ian Sharman

Hardback: ISBN 978-1-916968-42-4
eBook: ISBN 978-1-916968-43-1

For Markosia Enterpises Ltd:

Harry Markos
Publisher & Managing Partner

GM Jordan
Special Projects Co-Ordinator

Andy Briggs
Creative Consultant

Ian Sharman
Editor In Chief

The Sphinxing Rabbit

Madame Budgie Dots and The Dainty Dotes on Nodes Salon

Written by Pauline Chakmakjian
Illustrated by Nilesh Mistry

The Sphinxing Rabbit was
horrified by the gluttony
surrounding her.

The Duc de Bunny was equally horrified at the eyesore but not surprised since serfs in the fields toil away weight gain in fiefdoms.

The Sphinxing Rabbit made a speech
about Attractiveness Privilege and
expressed how disappointed she was
with everyone.

The inhabitants of the warren were
ashamed of themselves.

A gymnastics park was established for anyone who voluntarily wished to use it, but guarded by robots to assist with discipline.

For those willing, their exercise regime commenced so that they would slowly reverse the error of their ways.

But alas, it was already too late for the Ladybug.
It was with regret The Sphinxing Rabbit announced
the unfortunate passing due to obesity.

The Ladybug was buried in a mound
some distance from the warren, but it
was so big it served both as a memorial
and a reminder.

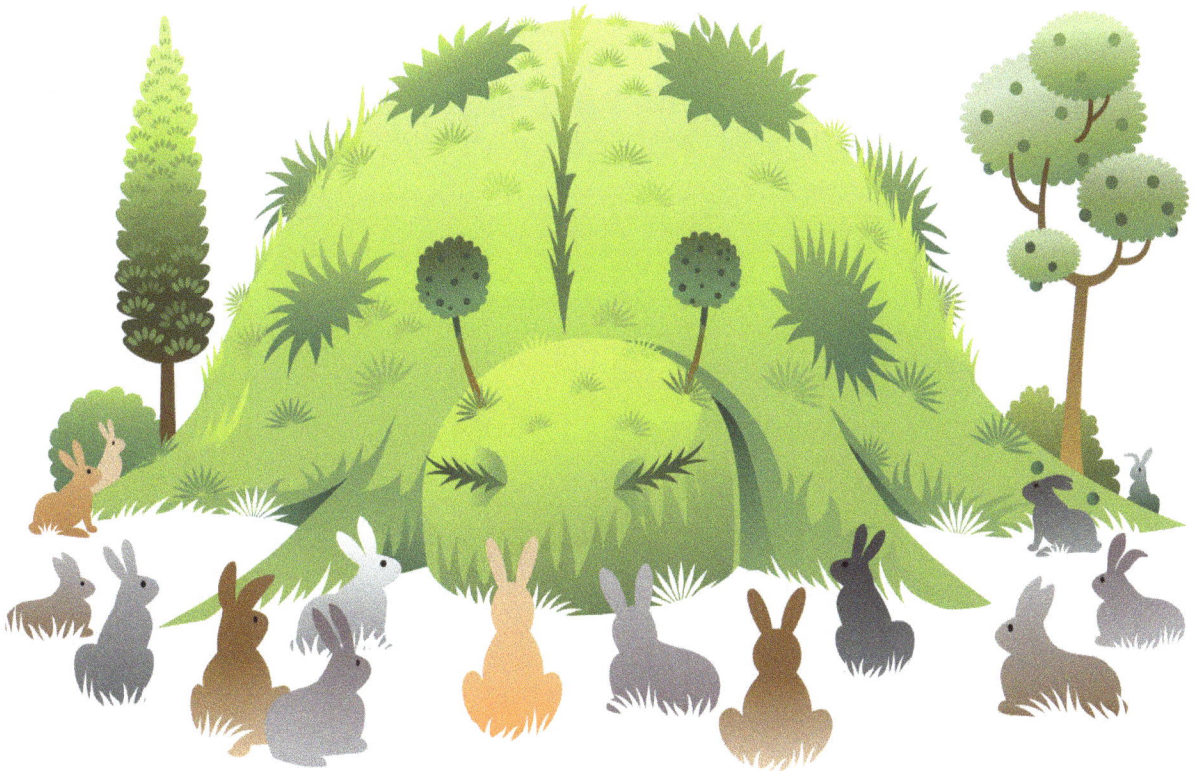

"Come away from the window, my dear," said the Duc de Bunny to The Sphinxing Rabbit.

"You know it's going to take a while before that eyesore disappears," he continued.

An hour later, the Duc de Bunny suggested to The Sphinxing Rabbit, "A distraction might be nice – perhaps your friend, Madame Budgie Dots?"

"Yes! Madame Budgie Dots, you really ought to meet her."

Madame Budgie Dots had just bid farewell to the last of her guests after a concert at her salon and she couldn't wait to greet The Sphinxing Rabbit and the Duc de Bunny.

She welcomed them with treats
and sweets.

"I'm so delighted you could visit me this evening – shame about your little, well, big friend," said Madame Budgie Dots.

"Yes, anyway, Her Sovereign Majesty has been telling me so much about you. If it's not too late in the evening, I'm intrigued by how you established such an elegant salon," said the Duc de Bunny.

Madame Budgie Dots explained
she would be happy to describe the
origins of her salon.

"Well, like a lot of talented songbirds, I was in a gilded cage."

"It was all rather confining. I
neither had much freedom nor
many choices."

"And, there were others more
powerful who controlled when to let
me out from time to time."

"I looked to the left, but saw
things so grotesque I moved back
to the center."

"I looked to the right, but that
was not much better, so I stayed
in the center again."

"I looked up above, but it was too
bright for me to see."

"I looked down below
and at least I could
see something."

"As above, so below,
as they say."

"Then, one evening I sang in a newly composed opera and an admirer of my coloratura requested an audience with me."

"He was a mysterious man
wearing a skull ring – I'd never
ventured out on a finger like that
before, so I hesitated."

"He invited me to step out of my cage permanently and, ever since, I've been free running this salon."

"Well, I shan't bore you further as you must wish to retire since it's rather late in the evening."

"Hmmm, how very fascinating, not a bore at all. We're so looking forward to attending some of your gatherings," said the Duc de Bunny to the charming Madame Budgie Dots.

"Oh, but if I may say so, you ought not to be dressed in those robes. Not to distress you or anything, but things just haven't been quite the same since 1789. I'll have my tailors create something suitable first thing in the morning."

34

The Sphinxing Rabbit explained to the
Duc de Bunny that it's best to blend in
as Madame Budgie Dots advised.

The Sphinxing Rabbit was gifted
a splendid pink dress.

The Duc de Bunny was gifted a magnificent blue ensemble.

A cordwainer had
also visited.

As did others for jewels, wigs and dainty
things so they were ready for things like…

40

The Dainty Dotes on Do's and Don'ts

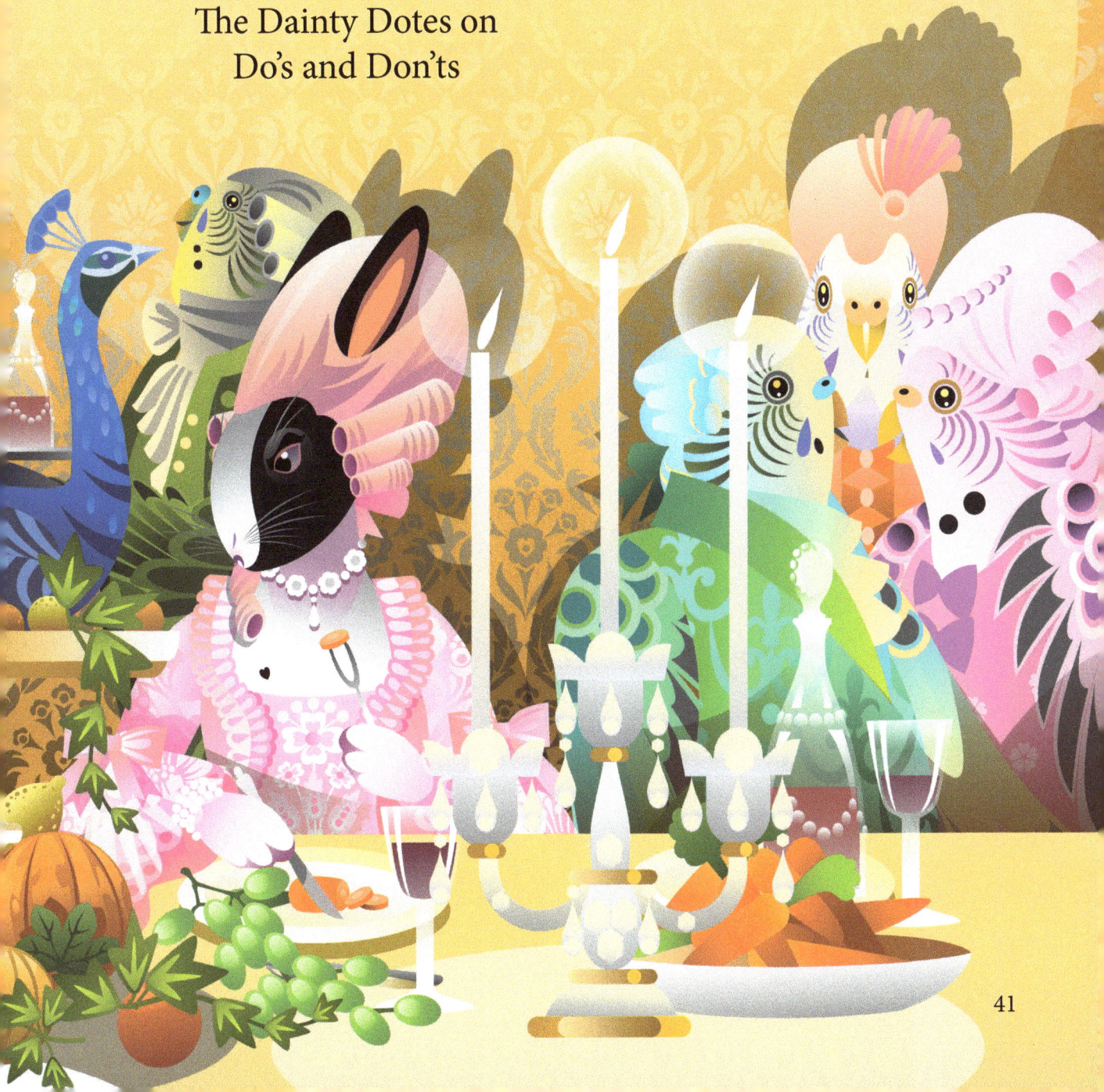

The Dainty Dotes
on Notes.

43

And the Dainty
Dotes on Antidotes.

Still in France, "I really ought to give you the third degree for not undergoing your rituals!" Madame Budgie Dots complained to The Sphinxing Rabbit, whimsically.

46

"Oh, yes, that's right. It's time I did do that," agreed The Sphinxing Rabbit.

47

And so, The Sphinxing Rabbit
completed her first masonic
degree at long last.

48

There was a celebratory
feast afterwards with the
lodge members.

"You really ought to consider it too, my dear Duke," suggested Madame Budgie Dots to the Duc de Bunny.

"It sounds most delightful but these
ladies do screech quite a lot. No offense,
dear Madame, but must it be *this* lodge?"
enquired the Duc de Bunny.

"None taken – I understand. I rather think you might enjoy a traditional, male-only British lodge," Madame Budgie Dots said, sympathetically.

"Yes, I think so too. My understanding is this sort of thing all started in France only a decade or so ago anyway," the Duc de Bunny speculated.

"Quite correct – it was thought
a rather gracious idea to have
ladies present."

"Rather a noisy idea if I
may say so," the irritated
Duc de Bunny said.

"Really! We'll sort it out in London, but for now at least try to enjoy the banquet," whispered The Sphinxing Rabbit to the Duc de Bunny.

"Please, it's all fine. A dear friend of mine was exactly the same. You'll meet him in London when we get there. He's well-placed to advise you on such matters in The City."

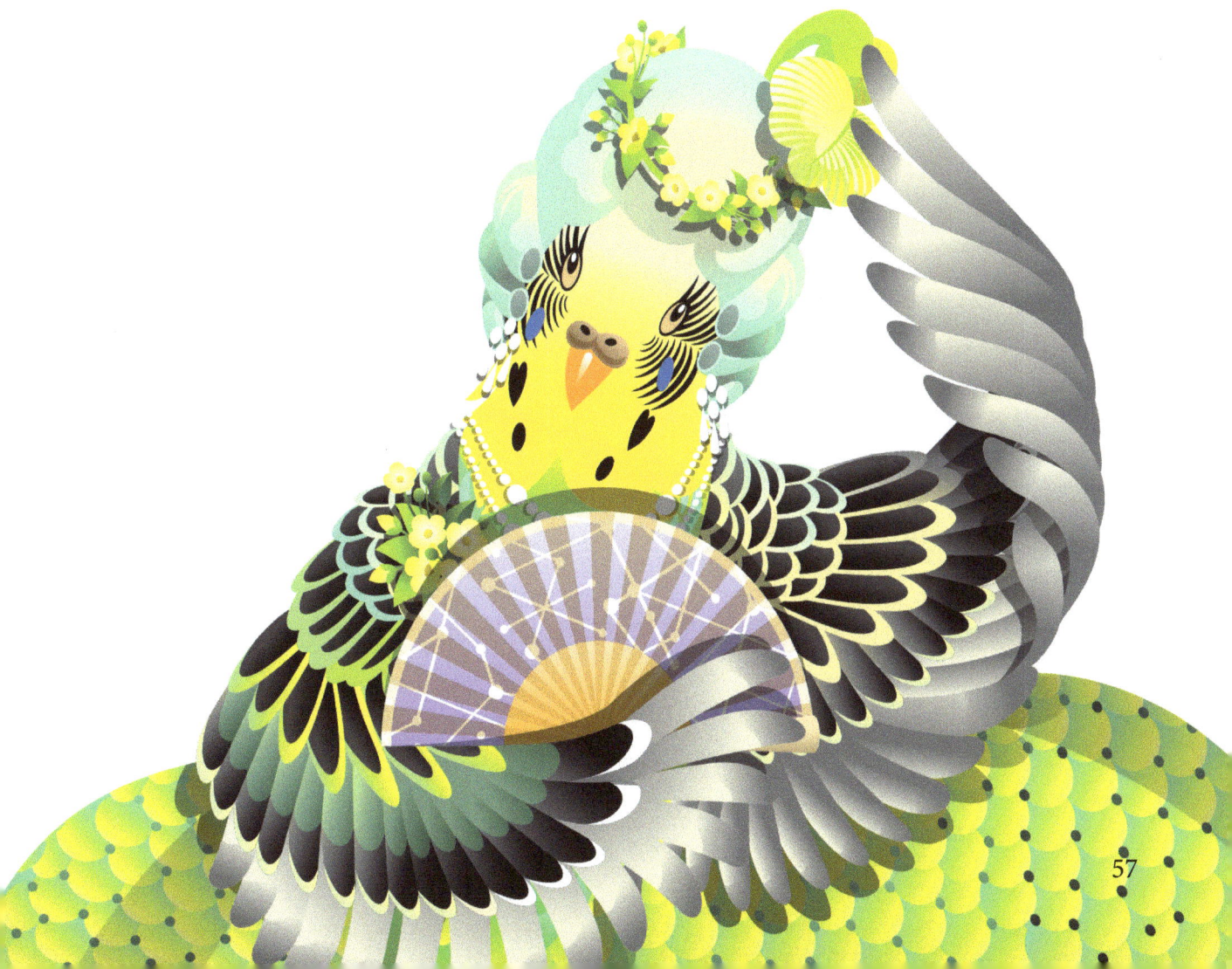

The very next day, all were
surprised to discover the time
machine was broken.

They decided to go to London with the time machine in the hot air balloon of Madame Budgie Dots to also see if it could be repaired there.

The next evening, they dined as guests of
The Lord Mayor of The City of London at
the Guildhall.

Enjoy London!

The End for Now.

Special thanks to
my father,
Dr. George Chakmakjian

Author

Pauline Chakmakjian is an author, artist, public speaker, advisor and a Freeman of the City of London.

Illustrator

Nilesh Mistry is an illustrator, designer and mural artist.
www.nileshmistry.com

www.ingramcontent.com/pod-product-compliance
Lightning Source LLC
Chambersburg PA
CBHW040849100426
42813CB00015B/2750